A Treasury of Thrift

Save Money with Frugal Wisdom from the Past

Compiled by Hugh Morrison

Montpelier Publishing
London
2015

ISBN-13: 978-1508994510
ISBN-10: 150899451X
Published by Montpelier Publishing, London.
Printed by Amazon Createspace.
First Kindle edition 2013.
Cover image © Fotolia

Contents

Introduction

Since the global financial crisis struck in 2008, more and more people have had to economise and find ways of cutting back on spending, and in countries such as the United Kingdom where interest rates are at an all time low, they also need to find more ways to make their savings grow. The internet is awash with websites and e-books on how to save money, but most of these concentrate on the details of how to save, rather than the theory.

Whilst this is all good advice, it is a bit like telling an alcoholic how to buy his whisky more cheaply. Someone who is serious about saving needs what some on Martin Lewis's excellent website 'Moneysaving Expert' call a 'lightbulb moment' – the realisation that their whole approach has to change; and this requires a philosophical shift.

From time immemorial there have been writers on thrift, but the first great writers on this theme, such as Benjamin Franklin, began to emerge in the eighteenth century. As literacy and cheap printing spread in the nineteenth century, a wealth of thrifty writing was produced. This little book aims to summarise those theories.

It is not a book of detailed hints. Old books are full of ideas using materials which aren't available any more to solve a problem which no longer exists. You know the kind of thing: 'to remove brilliantine stains from celluloid evening dress collars, take one ounce of sulphur with a tincture of potash and laudanum, and leave in the grate until the ashes be cold' etc. (Laudanum seemed to be the cure all for everything in the old days!) or even those which seem totally incomprehensible, eg 'Five cents' worth of tragaeanth will make more mucilage than 25 cents' worth of gum arable.'

I have therefore kept to broad and general theories to help the reader develop a thrifty philosophy; from then on he or she can look at moneysaving hints and tips in more detail.*A Treasury of Thrift* can be summarised as follows using these well worn sayings:

- Spend less than you earn
- Work smarter, not harder
- Neither a borrower nor a lender be
- From little acorns, great oak trees grow
- Penny wise is pound foolish

There are those who say (the author Jack London was one of them) that thrift is something akin to a sticking plaster on a gaping wound; that our entire economic system needs to change. That is as may be; but since London's time, attempts at systemic change have not proved successful, and for the time being, those struggling financially have to get their own house in order before attempting to change the world.

Present day economists also like to talk about the 'paradox of thrift', ie that thrift harms the economy because people spend less. My view is that it does no good to tell those struggling financially that they should spend what they do not have to help the economy; that only enriches their creditors.

The books quoted from range from those which advocate a simple life with very little need for money or business; almost an escape from the entire financial system, such as *Walden* or the *Quest for the Simple Life*, through to those which are explicitly aimed at capitalists wishing to build wealth and businesses, such as *The Art of Money Getting*. The modern reader will hopefully choose the middle way and achieve a balance, by accruing money through thrift and using it wisely and generously.

This is a companion volume to *Frontier Frugal*, also available for Kindle. Whilst this book introduces the philosophy of old-style money saving, *Frontier Frugal* gives you practical household hints to put those theories into action.

I hope you will find this collection of the thrifty sages of the past useful and that you will be inspired to read some of the works in full.

Thrifty theories

Be frugal and free. *Benjamin Franklin.*

Thrift comes too late when you find it at the bottom of your purse.
Seneca

Thrift teaches how to spend as well as how to save. Many people have
accumulated money who do not know how to spend it wisely.
Orison Swett Marden

There is that scattereth, and yet increaseth; and there is that
withholdeth more than is meet, but it tendeth to poverty.
Proverbs

Thrift is not in any way connected with avarice, usury, greed, or
selfishness. It is, in fact, the very reverse of these disgusting
dispositions.
Samuel Smiles

Thrift is the making the best of what one has in strength, time, or
money; getting one hundred per cent, in one's relations with life.
Thrift is an appreciation and application of the accumulative force of
little things. Thrift is a constructive force; waste is its destructive
opposite. Sometimes thrift is saving, going without; sometimes thrift is
spending – 'there is a scattering that increaseth' – but always it is
something for something.
Dora Morrell Hughes

I knew that I was not the gainer by a larger income, if I could buy a
more real satisfaction on less income. I saw that it was the artificial

needs of life that made me a slave; the real needs of life were few.
William J Dawson

We have said that thrift began with civilization: we might almost have said that thrift produced civilization.
Samuel Smiles

...it is not the high cost of living, but the cost of living high, that cripples so many lives...
Orison Swett Marden

...it is not the high cost of living, but the cost of living high, that cripples so many lives...

Most of the luxuries, and many of the so-called comforts of life, are not only not indispensable, but positive hindrances to the elevation of mankind.
Henry Thoreau

True economy consists in always making the income exceed the out-go. Wear the old clothes a little longer if necessary; dispense with the new pair of gloves; mend the old dress: live on plainer food if need be; so that, under all circumstances, unless some unforeseen accident occurs, there will be a margin in favour of the income. A penny here, and a dollar there, placed at interest, goes on accumulating, and in this way the desired result is attained.
PT Barnum

Comparatively few people can be rich; but most have it in their power to acquire, by industry and economy, sufficient to meet their personal wants.
Samuel Smiles

Frugality may be termed the daughter of Prudence, the sister of Temperance, and the parent of Liberty. He that is extravagant will quickly become poor, and poverty will enforce dependence, and invite corruption; it will almost always produce a passive compliance with the wickedness of others; and there are few who do not learn by degrees to practise those crimes which they cease to censure.
Samuel Johnson

...true thrift is getting the proportion of most for the expenditure, not the price.

The foundation of true thrift is getting the proportion of most for the expenditure, not the price. One does not learn this relation all at once or by accident, but by computation. Once learned you may build on it your home of thrift.
Dora Morrell Hughes

The old suit of clothes, and the old bonnet and dress, will answer for another season; the Croton or spring water taste better than champagne; a cold bath and a brisk walk will prove more exhilarating than a ride in the finest coach; a social chat, an evening's reading in the family circle, or an hour's play of 'hunt the slipper' and 'blind man's buff' will be far more pleasant than a fifty or five hundred dollar party, when the reflection on the difference in cost is indulged in by those who begin to know the pleasures of saving.
PT Barnum

It should be perfectly clear that thrift does not mean the hoarding of money. To hoard money is one of the most thriftless things one can do with it. The miser of romance who kept his money in a secret hoard where he might gloat over it and enjoy the sensations of feeling, hearing and seeing it was, in the strictest possible sense, a thriftless consumer of wealth.
Carver Thomas Nixon

If you are a thrifty person you are happy. When you are earning more than you spend, when you produce more than you consume, your life is a success, and you are filled with courage, animation, ambition, good-will. The world is beautiful, for the world is your view of the world, and when you are right with yourself, all's right with the world.
Elbert Hubbard

True economy is a careful treasurer in the service of benevolence; and where they are united respectability, prosperity and peace will follow.
Lydia Maria Frances Child

Thrift does not require superior courage, nor superior intellect, nor any superhuman virtue. It merely requires common sense, and the power of resisting selfish enjoyments. In fact, thrift is merely common sense in every-day working action.
Orison Swett Marden

Superfluous wealth can buy superfluities only. Money is not required to buy one necessary of the soul.
Henry Thoreau

The scantiest crop, if managed with frugality and economy, will maintain through the year the same number of people that are commonly fed on a more affluent manner by one of moderate plenty.
Adam Smith

6

All of us covet some neighbour's possession, and think our lot would have been happier, had it been different from what it is. Yet most of us could obtain worldly distinctions, if our habits and inclinations allowed us to pay the immense price at which they must be purchased. True wisdom lies in finding out all the advantages of a situation in which we *are* placed, instead of imagining the enjoyments of one in which we are *not* placed.
Lydia Maria Frances Child

...all pleasure in money ends at the point where economy becomes unnecessary.

Riches and happiness have no necessary connection with each other. In some cases it might be said that happiness is in the inverse proportion to riches. The happiest part of most men's lives is while they are battling with poverty, and gradually raising themselves above it.
Samuel Smiles

However mean your life is, meet it and live it; do not shun it and call it hard names. It is not so bad as you are. It looks poorest when you are richest.
Henry Thoreau

The thing that is least perceived about wealth is that all pleasure in money ends at the point where economy becomes unnecessary. The man who can buy anything he covets, without any consultation with his banker, values nothing that he buys.
William J Dawson

Thrift of Time is equal to thrift of money.
Samuel Smiles

> *It is not what a man gets that constitutes his wealth, but his manner of spending and economizing.*

Economy is generally despised as a low virtue, tending to make people ungenerous and selfish. This is true of avarice; but it is not so of economy. The man who is economical, is laying up for himself the permanent power of being useful and generous.
Lydia Maria Frances Child

I was rich, if not in money, in sunny hours and summer days, and spent them lavishly; nor do I regret that I did not waste more of them in the workshop or the teacher's desk.
Henry Thoreau

It is not wealth that gives the true zest to life, - but reflection, appreciation, taste, culture.
Samuel Smiles

An ounce of brains is worth a pound of money in achieving success...money can be lost with startling rapidity; it's seldom that a man loses his intelligence. Brain power evolves proper methods, and right methods make money.
Teller and Brown

Thrift began with civilization. It began when men found it necessary to provide for to-morrow, as well as for to-day. It began long before money was invented.
Samuel Smiles

It is not what a man gets that constitutes his wealth, but his manner of spending and economizing.
Samuel Smiles

The species of economy which is of general use is a judicious adaptation of expenditure to income...and not the constant struggle to diminish expenses, and to save in every iota.
Mrs William Parkes

Without frugality none can be rich, and with it very few would be poor.
Samuel Johnson

Thrifty saving

Not to have a mania for buying, is to possess a revenue.
Cicero

A man who both spends and saves money is the happiest man,
because he has both enjoyments.
Samuel Johnson

The want of parsimony in time of peace imposes the necessity of
contracting debt in time of war.
Adam Smith

Stinginess is selfishness. If you notice, you will find the givers among
the thrifty. What they have not wasted they share with others.
Dora Morrell Hughes

There is no thrift in saving when the value of the article saved is less
than the expense of saving it. Sometimes there is more thrift in
throwing away than in saving.
Dora Morrell Hughes

By no means run in debt: take thine own measure
Who cannot live on twenty pounds a year
Cannot on forty: he's a man of pleasure
A kind of thing that's for itself too dear.
George Herbert

The rich ruleth over the poor, and the borrower is servant to the
lender.
Proverbs

The chief discovery which I have made is that man may lead a perfectly honourable, sufficing, and even joyous existence upon a very small income.
William J Dawson

To save money for avaricious purposes is altogether different from saving it for economical purposes. The saving may be accomplished in the same manner - by wasting nothing, and saving everything. But here the comparison ends. The miser's only pleasure is in saving. The prudent economist spends what he can afford for comfort and enjoyment, and saves a surplus for some future time.
Samuel Smiles

In trying to economize in petty ways thousands of men fail to do the bigger things possible for them...You cannot afford to economize at the expense of mental strength, at the expense of efficiency.
Orison Swett Marden

It is the character of true economy to be as comfortable and genteel with a little, as others can be with much. *Lydia Maria Frances Child*

Go to the ant, thou sluggard; consider her ways, and be wise: which having no guide, overseer, or ruler, provideth her meat in the summer, and gathereth her food in the harvest.
Proverbs

If any persons think some of the maxims too rigidly economical, let them inquire how the largest fortunes among us have been made. They will find thousands and millions have been accumulated by a scrupulous attention to sums infinitely more minute than sixty cents.
Lydia Maria Frances Child

The first step toward independence is the limitation of our wants. We must be fed, clothed, and lodged in such a way that a self-respecting life is possible to us; when we have ascertained the figure at which this ideal can be realised, we have ascertained the price of independence.
William J Dawson

Paper money is in itself so easy a thing to create that its use often engenders the idea that wealth itself may be ground out of a paper-mill. In this country this delusive idea has of late years gained a much firmer foothold than many people think, and under the stimulus given to speculation by the use of our depreciated and irredeemable paper, schemes of all sorts have been set on foot, most of them seeming safe and honest enough, but all of them designed in one way or another to create wealth out of nothing, by means of bonds and stocks and mortgages.
George Carey Eggleston

> *The first step toward independence is the limitation of our wants.*

Cannot people realize how large an income is thrift?
Cicero

Thrifty spending

The methods of practising economy are very simple. Spend less than you earn. That is the first rule.
Samuel Smiles

Buy what thou hast no need of, and ere long thou shalt sell thy necessaries.
Benjamin Franklin

The methods of practising economy are very simple. Spend less than you earn. That is the first rule.

Thrift, no less than extravagance, consists in using money — that is, in spending it. The sole difference is in the purpose or purposes for which it is used or spent.

To spend money for immediate and temporary gratification is extravagance. To spend it for things which add to one's power, mental, physical, moral or economic, is thrift.
Carver Thomas Nixon

...it is wiser to buy regularly at the same stores than to wander about looking for bargains. Very often so-called bargains have short weight or other weaknesses.
Dora Morrell Hughes

We are taxed quite as much by our idleness, three times as much by our pride, and four times as much by our folly; and from these taxes the Commissioners cannot ease or deliver us by allowing an abatement.
Benjamin Franklin

Many persons are diligent enough in making money, but do not know how to economize it,--or how to spend it. They have sufficient skill and industry to do the one, but they want the necessary wisdom to do the other.
Samuel Smiles

The liberal soul shall be made fat: and he that watereth shall be watered also himself.
Proverbs

A bargain seldom answers; it is far from being economical to buy things the value of which is depreciated; and the remark of a friend of mine with regard to cheap goods is just: 'I cannot afford,' says he, 'to purchase them'.
Mrs Parkes Williams

It is not what you pay that makes the important factor in living but what you get for what you pay.
Dora Morrell Hughes

The use of money is all the advantage there is in having money.
Benjamin Franklin

He that kills a breeding sow destroys all her offspring to the thousandth generation. He that murders a crown (25p) destroys all that might have produced even scores of pounds.
Benjamin Franklin

One may be polite and kind towards others, without a penny in the purse. Politeness goes very far; yet it costs nothing.
Samuel Smiles

Make no expense but to do good today.
Benjamin Franklin

I calculated that out of a nominal income of 250 pounds per annum 100 pounds was paid as a tax to convention and respectability.
William J Dawson

Out of 250 pounds, 100 pounds was paid as a tax to convention and respectability.

People of the highest position, in point of culture and education, have often as great privations to endure as the average of working people. They have often to make their incomes go much further. They have to keep up a social standing. They have to dress better; and live sufficiently well for the purpose of health.

Though their income may be less than that of colliers and iron-workers, they are under the moral necessity of educating their sons and bringing them up as gentlemen, so that they may take their fair share of the world's work.
Samuel Smiles

It seems to me that money has lost more than half its value since cheques became common. When men kept their gold in iron coffers, lock-fast cupboards, or a pot buried in an orchard, there was something tangible in wealth. When it came to counting out gold pieces in a bag, men remembered by what sweat of mind or body

wealth was won, and they had a sense of parting with something which was really theirs.
William J Dawson

Without economy, a man cannot be generous. He cannot take part in the charitable work of the world. If he spends all that he earns, he can help nobody.
Samuel Smiles

The average citizen, if he did but know it, is always buying money too dear. He earns, let us say, four hundred pounds a year; but the larger proportion of this sum goes in what is called 'keeping up appearances.'
William J Dawson

What madness it is to run in debt for superfluities! We buy fine articles - finer than we can pay for. We are offered six months'- twelve months' credit! It is the shopkeeper's temptation; and we fall before it. We are too spiritless to live upon our own earnings; but must meanwhile live upon others'. The Romans regarded their servants as their enemies. One might almost regard modern shopkeepers in the same light.
Samuel Smiles

Do not trouble yourself much to get new things, whether clothes or friends. Turn the old; return to them. Things do not change; we change. Sell your clothes and keep your thoughts.
Henry Thoreau

The thrifty home

A healthy home, presided over by a thrifty, cleanly woman, may be the abode of comfort, of virtue, and of happiness.
Samuel Smiles

There is nothing in which the extravagance of the present day strikes me so forcibly as the manner in which our young people of moderate fortune furnish their houses.
Lydia Maria Francis Child

American households as a whole have been managed as if to use no more than was needed, to save the bit here and there, were beneath their dignity.
Dora Morrell Hughes

How beautiful and yet how cheap are flowers.
Samuel Smiles

That there are so many who feel time spent in work at home to be time wasted explains in a large part why the cost of living has steadily increased. All waste raises the cost of living.
Dora Morrell Hughes

Thrift is the spirit of order applied to domestic management and organization. Its object is to manage frugally the resources of the family; to prevent waste; and avoid useless expenditure. Thrift is under the influence of reason and forethought, and never works by chance or by fits. It endeavours to make the most and the best of everything. It does not save money for saving's sake.
Samuel Smiles

If it costs a man fifty pounds a year more to live in London than in the country, he is obviously no better off by the extra fifty pounds he earns in London. He is not earning fifty pounds for himself but fifty pounds for the landlord, the rate-collector, the gas-man, the restaurant proprietor, the omnibus and railway companies. His gold never reaches his own pocket; it is filched from him by dexterous thieves...
William J Dawson

Keeping up appearances is one of the great social evils of the age.

Keeping up appearances is one of the greatest social evils of the age. There is a general effort, more particularly amongst the middle and upper classes, at seeming to be something that they are not. They put on appearances, live a life of sham, and endeavour to look something superior to what they really are.
Samuel Smiles

A snug and a clean home, no matter how tiny it be, so that it be wholesome; windows into which the sun can shine cheerily; a few good books (and who need be without a few good books in these days of universal cheapness?) - no duns* at the door, and the cupboard well supplied, and with a flower in your room! There is none so poor as not to have about him these elements of pleasure.
Samuel Smiles

* debt collectors

In modern civilised life we get too many things done for us, and this is not merely an economical but an ethical mistake. It is difficult to feel any real pride in a home which is the creation of other people. In a true state of civilisation no man will pay another to do what he can do himself. Not only does he preserve his independence by such a rule, but he creates a hundred new objects of interest for himself.
William J Dawson

The true economy of housekeeping is simply the art of gathering up all the fragments, so that nothing be lost. I mean fragments of *time*, as well as materials. *Lydia Maria Francis Child*

We have an English proverb that says, 'He that would thrive, must ask his wife.' It was lucky for me that I had one as much dispos'd to industry and frugality as myself. She assisted me chearfully in my business... We kept no idle servants, our table was plain and simple, our furniture of the cheapest. *Benjamin Franklin*

> *The true economy of housekeeping is simply the art of gathering up all the fragments.*

I sat at a table where were rich food and wine in abundance, and obsequious attendance, but sincerity and truth were not; and I went away hungry from the inhospitable board.
Henry Thoreau

It is not necessary that a picture should be high-priced in order to be beautiful and good.
Samuel Smiles

So sure is it that the love and culture of flowers lead to prosperity that in proportion as the love for a few potted plants and flowers at home increases so the waste of money on meretricious ornament is checked or stopped. The education absorbed by the eye is of great importance, and flowers and plants instruct as no text-books ever can.
Robert McMeans

The thrifty kitchen

A fat kitchen makes a lean will.
Benjamin Franklin

In criticism of our American housewives it has been said over and over again that a French housewife would feed a family on what an average family throws away.
Orison Swett Marden

The poor man who roasts or broils his meat- throws it half into the fire.
The poor man who boils it throws half away in the water.
The poor man who turns it into broth with a little flour, oatmeal, rice, or pease, according to their price, wants the less bread, and has twice the quantity for his money.
Bob Short

Large families serve thrift by buying in quantity, but small families living in flats may find quantity-buying very wasteful. For a large family to buy flour by the bag is as foolish as for a small family to buy it by the barrel.
Dora Morrell Hughes

The art of living extends to all the economies of the household. It selects wholesome food, and serves it with taste. There is no profusion; the fare may be very humble, but it has a savour about it; everything is so clean and neat, the water so sparkles in the glass, that you do not desire richer viands, or a more exciting beverage.
Samuel Smiles

I learned from my two years' experience that it would cost incredibly little trouble to obtain one's necessary food, even in this latitude; that a

man may use as simple a diet as the animals, and yet retain health and strength. I have made a satisfactory dinner, satisfactory on several accounts, simply off a dish of purslane (*Portulaca oleracea*) which I gathered in my cornfield, boiled and salted.
Henry Thoreau

We see so many women in England, who seem to know no more of the constituent parts of a loaf than they know of those of the moon. Servant women in abundance appear to think that loaves are made by the baker, as knights are made by the king; things of their pure creation, a creation, too, in which no one else can participate. Now, is not this an enormous evil?
William Cobbett

Another great waste for the consumer has developed from what is said to be a commendable measure, that is, the fancy box and carton business. This is claimed to be more sanitary, and so it is in a few instances, but as a whole it is a claim unjustified by facts, and a decided item in increasing the cost of living.
Dora Morrell Hughes

In short, we want common sense in cookery, as in most other things. Food should be used, and not abused. Much of it is now absolutely wasted, wasted for want of a little art in cooking it. Food is not only wasted by bad cooking; but much of it is thrown away which French women would convert into something savoury and digestible. Health, morals, and family enjoyments, are all connected with the question of cookery. Above all, it is the handmaid of Thrift.
Samuel Smiles

(*home brewing of beer*) will be found to be so easy a thing, that I am not without hope, that many tradesmen, who now spend their evenings at the public house, amidst tobacco smoke and empty noise, may be induced, by the finding of better drink at home, at a quarter

part of the price, to perceive that home is by far the pleasantest place wherein to pass their hours of relaxation.
William Cobbett

The principal meal of a Guernsey farmer consists of *soupe a la graisse*, which is, being interpreted, cabbage and peas stewed with a little dripping. This is the daily dinner of men who own perhaps three or four cows, a pig or two, and poultry. But the produce and the flesh of these creatures they sell in the market, investing their gains in extension of land, or stock.
Samuel Smiles

> *A pound of oatmeal contains twice as much of the same kind of nutrition as lean steak*

A pound of oatmeal contains twice as much of the same kind of nutrition as a pound of lean steak. Yet the one costs six cents, while the other costs two or three times as much.
Robert McMeans

Less meat is eaten when soup is served, and the body thrives as well. As a rule, the ordinary household does not serve soups as a first course of a dinner, seeming to regard it as a luxury for the table of the rich, whereas it is one of the greatest economies. It is rarely necessary to buy material for the daily soup.
Dora Morrell Hughes

Wealth is not necessary for comfort. Luxury requires wealth, but not comfort. A poor man's home, moderately supplied with the

necessaries of life, presided over by a cleanly, frugal housewife, may contain all the elements of comfortable living.
Samuel Smiles

If you want to know what your thrift amounts to in dollars and cents, try putting in a penny bank whatever is represented by the food you do not waste. You will thus get a realizing sense what thrift means. You will not have gone without any of the foods you wanted, but you will have made them of greater value to the family treasury.
Dora Morrell Hughes

To go without meat is no hardship after one gets into the habit, and thousands live healthfully and contentedly without any meat day after day. They feel better without it. Eating is largely a matter of habit.
Dora Morrell Hughes

Waste in the kitchen is often very great from apparently trivial sources. Housekeepers should read and ponder:

In cooking meats, the water is thrown out without removing the grease, or the grease from the dripping-pan is thrown away.
Pieces of bread in the bread-box, and cake in the cake-box are left to dry and mould.
Scraps of meat are thrown away.
Cold potatoes are left to sour and spoil.
Preserves are opened, forgotten, and left to mould and ferment.
Dried fruits are not looked after, and become wormy.
Vinegar and sauce are left standing in tin.
Apples are left to decay for want of 'sorting over.'
Corks are left out of the molasses and vinegar jugs.
The tea-canister is left open.
Victuals are left exposed to be eaten by mice.
Bones of meat and the carcass of turkey are thrown away, when they could be used in making good soups.
Vegetables and puddings left from the dinner are thrown away.
Sugar, tea, coffee, and rice are carelessly spilled in the handling.

Soap is left to dissolve and waste in the water.
Dish-towels are used for dish-cloths.
Towels are used for holders.
Brooms and mops are not hung up.
Robert McMeans

Thrifty health and wellbeing

Happiness is a mental attitude, it is the condition of the mind, not the condition of the pocketbook.
Orison Swett Marden

You will find it chemically true that five long, deep, well appropriated inspirations of pure air, are more invigorating than a cup of either wine, brandy, or coffee.
Robert McMeans

The habit of thrift proves your power to rule your own psychic self

The habit of thrift proves your power to rule your own psychic self. You are the captain of your soul. You are able to take care of yourself, and then out of the excess of your strength you produce a surplus.
Elbert Hubbard

A glass of pure cold water (not ice water), swallowed just before retiring at night, and another immediately upon arising in the morning, is an excellent thing for cleansing the stomach of impurities and keeping it healthy. Be temperate in all things, and health and happiness will be yours.
Robert McMeans

If people would stop taking medicine, pay a little more attention, to diet, exercise and care of the health, the patent medicine concerns would have to move to a new country for victims, but most people are of the idea that health can be bought for a dollar, in a big bottle, and the bigger the bottle the more health.
Robert McMeans

The habit of thrift tends to give clear eyes, good digestion, efficient muscles. People on moderate salaries have no business to patronize taxicabs.
Elbert Hubbard

Stuffing the pocketbook and starving the mind is pretty poor business.

Stuffing the pocketbook and starving the mind is pretty poor business.
Orison Swett Marden

Do not allow anyone to persuade you that your restoration can be bottled up and taken with a teaspoon. Food; rest; exercise: sunlight; fresh air: enthusiasm; these are the things that will cure you, if anything.
Robert McMeans

Many a man who is economical to stinginess in money matters, squanders with fearful prodigality his physical, mental, and moral energy and his time. He scorns a vacation, considering it a frightful waste of precious hours, loses needed sleep in working late at night at his desk, and is indifferent to regularity in eating. Such men pay the penalty in lowered vitality and a shortened business career.
Orison Swett Marden

One reason why animals and so-called savages have better health than civilized people is because they always attend promptly to their calls of nature: 'When Nature calls at either door/Do not try to bluff her/But haste away, whether night or day/Or health is sure to suffer.'
Robert McMeans

An ugly mood of mind makes us sick and loses us both friends and money, while a cheerful, loving disposition attracts help from many quarters.
Robert McMeans

The thrifty wardrobe

It is an interesting question how far men would retain their relative rank if they were divested of their clothes. Could you, in such a case, tell surely of any company of civilized men which belonged to the most respected class?
Henry Thoreau

Do not be content to wear silks and diamonds on the body...and to dress the mind in calico and the character in rags. Let self-improvement, self-culture, a healthy mind and a fine personality be your richest dress.
Orison Swett Marden

A patch on your coat and money in your pocket is better and more creditable than a writ on your back...

On the way to my office the tailor took toll of me by forcing me to wear a garb which I detested, simply because I dared wear no other garb.
William J Dawson

A patch on your coat and money in your pocket is better and more creditable than a writ on your back and no money to take it off.
Benjamin Franklin

One of the most profitable forms of thrift is to have street gowns for the street only, removing as soon as one gets home.
Dora Morrell Hughes

No good wife will ever consent to wear clothes and give dinners that belong not to her, but to her shopkeeper.
Samuel Smiles

Things that should be expensive look the cheapest and commonest of everything when bought in imitation or in cheap quality, and are really very dear because they do not last.
Dora Morrell Hughes

No man ever stood the lower in my estimation for having a patch in his clothes; yet I am sure that there is greater anxiety, commonly, to have fashionable, or at least clean and unpatched clothes, than to have a sound conscience.
Henry Thoreau

> *No good wife will ever consent to wear clothes and give dinners that belong not to her, but to her shopkeeper.*

Care of clothing is true thrift, and more important to one who would look well on a small amount than the original buying, for it not only doubles the life of a garment but keeps it looking well as long as anything of it is left.
Dora Morrell Hughes

A woman of limited means is well aware of the possibilities of a black dress. Such a dress can be worn upon almost any occasion.
Robert McMeans

It is more manly, as well as wiser, to dress less genteelly than your fellows, to live in a cheaper house than they, and to practice economies they never dream of practising, than to wrap yourself in lies as you do whenever you put on clothes which you cannot afford, or in any other way spend more than your income justifies you in spending, merely for the sake of conforming to the customs of those about you.

George Carey Eggleston

Thrift does not wait until everything has been worn thin before buying new, but gets a few things as the year goes by. It costs much more to make good the neglect of several years.
Dora Morrell Hughes

Thrifty business

Nothing makes a business man so absolutely independent as ready cash.
Orison Swett Marden

Every business man must be systematic and orderly...with persons of moderate means, the necessity for the eye of the master overlooking everything, is absolutely necessary for the proper conduct of business.
Samuel Smiles

He that riseth late must trot all day, and shall scarce overtake his business at night.

He that riseth late must trot all day, and shall scarce overtake his business at night; while laziness travels so slowly that poverty soon overtakes him.
Benjamin Franklin

I know a business man who makes his employees, as a matter of principle, save the string from packages, even if it takes twice as much time as the string is worth. This man, also, in trying to save electricity, keeps his place of business so dark and dingy that he loses custom. He does not realize that a good light is the best kind of advertisement.
Orison Swett Marden

The eye of the master will do more work than both his hands.
Benjamin Franklin

Let us take the life of the average business man by way of example....He gets a living, and perhaps in time an ample living; but does he live?
William J Dawson

For which of you, intending to build a tower, sitteth not down first, and counteth the cost, whether he have sufficient to finish it? Lest haply, after he hath laid the foundation, and is not able to finish it, all that behold it begin to mock him, saying, this man began to build, and was not able to finish.
St Luke

> *No idle or thriftless man ever became great.*

Politeness and civility are the best capital ever invested in business. Large stores, gilt signs, flaming advertisements, will all prove unavailing if you or your employees treat your patrons abruptly.
PT Barnum

Extravagant habits are incompatible with the thrift necessary for success in any career. There must be an underlying, clean-cut thrift in the nature, a disposition to make the most of everything, and to make every dollar go as far as possible, and to save just as much as possible without pinching in one's comforts or being mean.
Orison Swett Marden

No idle nor thriftless man ever became great. It is amongst those who never lost a moment, that we find the men who have moved and advanced the world,- by their learning, their science, or their inventions.
Samuel Smiles

Men should be systematic in their business. A person who does business by rule, having a time and place for everything, doing his work promptly, will accomplish twice as much and with half the trouble of him who does it carelessly and slipshod.
PT Barnum

Some men have a foolish habit of telling their business secrets. If they make money they like to tell their neighbours how it was done. Nothing is gained by this, and ofttimes much is lost.
PT Barnum

The apostle Paul planted the knowledge of the Christian religion over half the Roman empire; yet he supported himself by tent-making, and not by collecting subscriptions.
Samuel Smiles

Extravagant habits are incompatible with the thrift necessary for success in any career.

If every child in America had a thorough business training, tens of thousands of promoters, longheaded, cunning schemers, who have thriven on the people's ignorance, would be out of an occupation. *Orison Swett Marden*

It is impossible to persuade the labourer that a pound a week in London is really less than fifteen shillings (75p) a week in the country.
William J Dawson

When I make up a package of engraved business cards for any of our salesmen, I affix to it a typed slip stating that each card cost just one cent. The adoption of this policy resulted in an annual saving of over one hundred dollars.
Teller and Brown

In order to secure my credit and character as a tradesman, I took care not only to be in reality industrious and frugal, but to avoid all appearances to the contrary. I drest plainly; I was seen at no places of idle diversion. I never went out a-fishing or shooting; a book, indeed, sometimes debauch'd me from my work, but that was seldom, snug, and gave no scandal; and, to show that I was not above my business, I sometimes brought home the paper I purchas'd at the stores thro' the streets on a wheelbarrow. Thus being esteem'd an industrious, thriving young man, and paying duly for what I bought, the merchants who imported stationery solicited my custom; others proposed supplying me with books, and I went on swimmingly.
Benjamin Franklin

> *I took care not only to be in reality industrious and frugal, but to avoid all appearances to the contrary.*

Rubber bands, pens, pencils, erasers — all these items I've figured individually; and our staff is thoroughly posted on the cost of each pen, pencil, etc. Equipped with this datum, they instinctively avoid waste. It's human nature. Translate merchandise into money, and the desired result is achieved. They don't require urging. The previous waste of supplies is eliminated. The total annual saving amounts to a goodly sum.
Teller and Brown

It is the man with the savings-bank habit who seldom gets laid off; he's the one who can get along without you, but you cannot get along without him.
Orison Swett Marden

One of the wisest and most thoroughly cultivated men whom I ever knew, retired before the age of fifty, from a profession in which he was making an enormous income, because, he said, he had got as much as he or any one belonging to him could want, and he did not see why he should sacrifice the rest of his life to money-getting.
Samuel Smiles

If you are not thrifty in your own affairs, if you are not businesslike in managing them, others will take it for granted that you will be inefficient in the handling of their affairs.
Orison Swett Marden

The thoughtless and spendthrift take no heed of experience , and make no better provision for the future.

Though trade has invariably its cycles of good and bad years, like the lean and fat kine in Pharaoh's dream- its bursts of prosperity, followed by glut, panic, and distress - the thoughtless and spendthrift take no heed of experience, and make no better provision for the future. *Samuel Smiles*

The rulings issued by the railroads are admittedly intricate and difficult to grasp. But a patient study of them brings its reward in the shape of worth-while savings. And I don't know of any easier method of saving money than to reduce your shipping charges by ascertaining the one best and cheapest method of packing.
Teller and Brown

No greater delusion ever crept into a rich woman's head than that wanton extravagance is justified on the ground that it gives employment.
Orison Swett Marden

From the time that credit first entered into commercial transactions until now, men have been busily endeavouring to create wealth out of nothing, and now and then theorists imagine that they have discovered how to accomplish it.

It is so easy to delude not one's neighbours only but oneself, as well with sophistical financial reasoning, that the danger is present wherever credit enters into business transactions, however honest and well-meaning the authors of the mischief may be.
George Carey Eggleston

The thrifty future

In early childhood, you lay the foundation of poverty or riches, in the habits you give your children.
Lydia Maria Frances Child

One of the most pathetic phases of American life is that so many people are leading unhappy, wretched lives because in their youth they were not taught how to finance themselves.
Orison Swett Marden

...so many people are leading unhappy, wretched lives because in their youth they were not taught how to finance themselves.

Let the people learn necessary knowledge; let them learn to count their fingers, and to count their money, before they are caring for the classics.
Samuel Johnson

Parents, make your girl self-reliant, so that men will know that she is not dependent upon any one of them for support, that she is perfectly capable not only of making a living, but of making a career of distinction.
Orison Swett Marden

With children it is very different. They have no inveterate habits to get rid of. They will, for the most part, do as they are taught. And they can be taught economy, just as they can be taught arithmetic. They can, at all events, be inspired by a clever

teacher with habits of economy and thrift.
Samuel Smiles

Every child should be started in life with a bank account, however small, and something should be constantly added to this sum, no matter how little, if for no other reason than to implant in his mind the idea of saving, and the larger idea of thrift.
Orison Swett Marden

Begin early is the great maxim for everything in education. A child of six years old can be made useful; and should be taught to consider every day lost in which some little thing has not been done to assist others.
Lydia Maria Frances Child

It is only when men become wise and thoughtful that they become frugal.

We find boys and girls turned out of school and college full of theories, and all sorts of smatterings of knowledge, but without the ability to protect themselves from human thieves who are trying to get something for nothing.
Orison Swett Marden

Those things for which the most money is demanded are never the things which the student most wants. Tuition, for instance, is an important item in the term bill, while for the far more valuable education which he gets by associating with the most cultivated of his contemporaries no charge is made.
Henry Thoreau

I would not that servile and laborious employment should be forced upon the young. I would merely have each one educated according to his probable situation in life; and be taught that whatever is his duty, is honourable; and that no merely external circumstance can in reality injure true dignity of character. I would not cramp a boy's energies by compelling him always to cut wood, or draw water; but I would teach him not to be ashamed, should his companions happen to find him doing either one or the other. *Lydia Maria Frances Child*

Considerable financial training may be obtained by girls in connection with household affairs. For example, a little girl of eleven, who had just baked her first batch of bread, figured out its cost in comparison with baker's bread...This shows that forty-five cents are saved by making bread at home, not counting the work and cost of baking.
Edwin A Kirkpatrick

It is only when men become wise and thoughtful that they become frugal. Hence the best means of making men and women provident is to make them wise.
Samuel Smiles

The girl or boy who acquires the habit of thrift early in life will be a power for good in any community.
Elbert Hubbard

Bibliography/suggested reading

Barnum, PT: *The Art of Money Getting, or Golden Rules for Making Money.* Paris, JS Brown, *1890.*

Child, Lydia Maria Frances: *The American Frugal Housewife.* New York, Samuel S and William Wood, 1838

Cobbett, William: *Cottage Economy.* New York, John Doyle, 1833. Dawson, William J: *The Quest of the Simple Life.* New York, EP Dutton, 1907.

Eggleston, George Carey: *How to make a living: suggestions on the art of making, saving and using money.* GP Putnam and Sons, New York, 1875.

Franklin, Benjamin: *The Way to Wealth, or Poor Richard Improved* (corrected and enlarged by Bob Short), London, W Darton, 1814.

Hubbard, Elbert: *Selected Writings of Elbert Hubbard.* New York, William H Wise and Co, 1922.

Hughes, Dora Morrell: *Thrift in the Household.* Boston, Lothrop, Lee, Shepard and Co, 1918.

Johnson, Samuel: various including *Journey to the Western Islands, The Rambler* and *Anecdotes of Dr Johnson.*

Kirkpatrick, Edwin A. The Use of Money: How to Save and How to Spend. Indianapolis, The Bobbs-Merrill Company, 1915.

Marden, Orison Swett. *Thrift.* New York, Thomas Y Crowell Company, 1918.

McMeans, Robert: *The Helper, a Help for those who wish to Save and Make Money and to Avoid Sickness.* Chicago, R McMeans, 1903.

Nixon, Carver Thomas: *War Thrift.* New York, Oxford University Press, 1919

Parkes Williams, Mrs: *Domestic Duties, or Instructions to Young Married Ladies on the Management of their Households.* New York, J and J Harper, 1829.

Porter, Mrs ME. *Mrs Porter's New Southern Cookbook and Companion for Frugal and Economical Householders.* John Potter and Sons, Philadelphia, 1871.

Smiles, Samuel: *Thrift.* London, John Murray, 1892.

Smith, Adam: *The Wealth of Nations.* London, JM Dent, 1910.

Teller, William Pierre and Brown, Henry Edwin: *Modern Business Methods.* Chicago, Rand McNally and Company, 1912

Thoreau, Henry: *Walden, or Life in the Woods.* Boston, Ticknor and Fields, 1854.

Various authors. *A Book of Practical Recipes for the Housewife.* Chicago Evening American. Date unknown.

Other titles from Montpelier Publishing
Available from Amazon

Frugal living and moneysaving
1001 Ways to Save Money: thrifty tips for the fabulously frugal!
A Treasury of Thrift: save money with frugal wisdom from the past
The Men's Guide to Frugal Grooming
The Frugal Gentleman: classic style for less money

Body, mind and spirit
Non-Religious Wedding Readings
The Simple Living Companion
Non-Religious Funeral Readings
Spiritual Readings for Funerals
Marriage Advice: Dos and Don'ts for Husbands and Wives

Humour and puzzles
Wedding Jokes: Hilarious Gags for your Best Man's Speech
The Book of Church Jokes: a Collection of (Mostly) Clean Christian
Chuckles
After Dinner Laughs: Jokes and Funny Stories for Speechmakers
After Dinner Laughs 2: More Jokes and Funny Stories
Scottish Jokes: a Wee Book of Clean Caledonian Chuckles
The Bumper Book of Riddles, Puzzles and Rhymes

Travel
The Dalai Lama Next Door: volunteering with Tibetans in
McLeodganj
The Slow Bicycle Companion: inspirational quotes from cycling's
golden age

Men's interest
The Pipe Smoker's Companion
Advice to Gentlemen
The Real Ale Companion
The Cigar Collection

Printed in the USA
CPSIA information can be obtained
at www.ICGtesting.com
LVHW050814280724
786599LV00002B/346

9 781508 994510